Hat

A ZEBRA BOOK

Written by David Lloyd
Illustrated by Gill Tomblin

PUBLISHED BY
WALKER BOOKS
LONDON

Sometimes you see a pink one,
floating through the fields.
'What's that?' you ask.
And Johnny Martin answers,
'That's my mum's hat!'

Sometimes you see a brown one,
coming down the street.
'What's that?' you ask.
And Johnny Martin answers,
'That's my dad's hat!'

Sometimes you see a straw one,
flying in the sky.
'What's that?' you ask.
And Johnny Martin answers,
'That's my sister Winnie's hat!'

Sometimes you see a knitted one,
on roller skates.
'What's that?' you ask.
And Johnny Martin answers,
'That's my brother Eric's hat!'

Sometimes you see a flat one,
walking the dog.
'What's that?' you ask.
And Johnny Martin answers,
'That's my grandad's hat!'

Sometimes you see a flowery one,
drinking a cup of tea.
'What's that?' you ask.
And Johnny Martin answers,
'That's my granny's hat!'

Mum.

Dad.

Winnie.

Eric.

Granny.   Grandad.

Johnny Martin.

'Just fancy that!' you say.
'Only Johnny Martin wears no hat!'

All together the Martins
climb into their car.

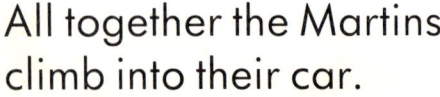

Only Johnny Martin wears no hat.

All together the Martins
arrive in the town.

Only Johnny Martin wears no hat.

All together the Martins
step inside the shop.

Only Johnny Martin wears no hat.

All together the Martins
push Johnny to the front.
'This is my Johnny,' says Dad.
'What he needs is a hat!'

A pink one.

A brown one.

A straw one

A flat one.

A flowery one.

A knitted one.

And now a cowboy one.
'What's that?' you ask.
And Johnny Martin answers,
'That's my Johnny Martin hat!'